MY LIFE'S
POETIC
Stories

INSPIRATIONAL

DONNA RICHTER

WESTBOW
PRESS®
A DIVISION OF THOMAS NELSON
& ZONDERVAN

WestBow Press books may be ordered through booksellers or by contacting:

WestBow Press
A Division of Thomas Nelson & Zondervan
1663 Liberty Drive
Bloomington, IN 47403
www.westbowpress.com
844-714-3454

ISBN: 978-1-6642-0354-9 (sc)
ISBN: 978-1-6642-0353-2 (e)

Print information available on the last page.

WestBow Press rev. date: 10/19/2020

CONTENTS

U.S. TROOPS READY FOR BATTLE

When the President Gives the "Go"
When All the Troops Then Head Over Seas
They Will Fight For Us All To Be Free
Aboard A Ship, On Land or Sea
The Troops Are Ready For What May Be
The Delays Are Over
Seriousness of War Is Just Hours Away
From U.S. Soldiers
It's Hard for Hearts to Accept Casualties
We Put Our Freedom in the U.S. Troop
And Abilities
More than Some of Our Soldiers
Are So Young, Some Eighteen
Some Just Twenty One
The More experienced, we are
Thankful For
They Taught Theses Men and Women
Just How to Even the Score
Weapons, Bombs, missiles Also, artillery
Anything I've forgotten? Or Have
Not Included?
Please Know Each One of You
Are Special To Me
For Our thoughts And Prayers Are Sent

You're Way
Protection Is In God's Hands
For He Is In command
No Matter What the Outcome Shall Be
There Is But One Ruler
For This One Knows Of Things
Before They Are To Happen
Our Thoughts Our Actions
Our Dreams Our Sorrows
Whose cheeks will dampen?
We Are "Proud To Be Americans"
Our Tribute We Give To All Our Troops
For The Fight That Is Needed
Stand Tall All You Who Are Serving Your Country
Move Ahead Now Godspeed
We Are Ready For Battle, All You Who Disobey
The Chances Are All Over to Us
Our Freedom Is Here To Stay
Victory Is Here To Stay Our Troops Will Not Give Up
Or Accept Any Other Outcome
God Protect All Who Serve
We Can Hear the Patriotic Songs Sung
From The U.S.Troops That Tell US
All about Them
We Love Our Troops
We Are Very Proud Of You
You're Braveness
Don't Ever Forget
The War Cannot Be Won Without You
We Depend On You to Save Us
"God Bless America, Home the Brave
Land Of the free"

ONCE UPON A CHILDHOOD LIFE

Once Upon A Time I Was Adolescent
Things Were Smooth Then
Not As Difficult As the Present

I Was Younger, Full Of Energy and Smiles
Life Was So Simple Then, No Worries
About Anything
This Feeling I should file

Now I've become a teen and how my life has changed
Things are not any Longer Simple
I can't Place the Blame n Anyone Else
These Feelings Feel So Strange

Mom and Dad Always Made Things All Better
When There Was a Problem
When There Was a Problem If I Was Hurt or Scared,
Sick or Upset, They'd find A Way to Calm Them

Now My Life Is More Difficult
All Changes and responsibilities
And Concerns Are All Upon Me
Although No Matter How Old You Are
Mom and Dad Will Always Be There
I seem to Forget When I Hurt Them
They Are Forgiving and Caring
They Look Past the Problem
And Do Spare Me

Sure I've Made Mistakes
For Becoming a Teen Has No Rulebook
To Pick Up and Find an Answer
By Searching the Index for the Right Chapter

Well Parents Didn't Have a Rulebook to Follow Either
We Have Huge Responsibilities
Also Problems to Absorb and Capture

So All in All Life Doesn't Seem So Fair Sometimes
To Any OF Us Really
But Remember We Are Human Beings
Rules Are Made and Broken
We Should Accept Life the Way It Is
By Forgiving Freely

We Love You Even When You Hurt Us
The Pain Goes Away Eventually
The Problem Diminishes In Time
That's the plus from Parenting
We love, Care, and Snap Back from These Wounds
Like The Spin of a Dime

Don't Subtract the Smiles Add Worries and Tears
For This Is Unbalanced Like a Fraction
The Decimal Is Moved Back And Forth
Out OF This Problem Comes Disrespect for Your Peers

We'll Always Love You Please Remember This
We'll End This Poem with a Hug and a Kiss
Love, Mom and Dad

A MILE OF HUGS

I Feel As Though People Who Can Hug
Are Very Strong People
Not Physically Of Course

Emotionally they are Telling You
They've Been There
They Feel This Feeling of Remorse

So If You Do Nothing Else This Week
Find Someone Who Needs a Hug

You'll Feel Good Too Knowing
You made a difference
Without A Word or a Tug

They'll Say "Thanks I Really Needed That"
Or Just Smile and Walk Away
But At Least You Know
You Made a Difference
What A Way to Begin Your Day

A SOLDIER

A Soldier Is Serving Our Country
The U.S.A. We Stand Proud Of The
Protection for Keeping Us Safe

Out on Missions Things Aren't So Easy
Not Sleeping In Beds
Temperatures Soaring To Over 100 Degrees
On Guard 24-7
Never A real Break

Heartaches of Missing Home, Family, And Friends
Wishing That This War in Iraq
Would Come To an End
Times Are Tough and We Know
You Put Your Lives on the Line

The Danger, the Losses, the Tears Hidden
But The Heart Breaks
Be Not Afraid To Cry

It Cleans the Soul
Let the Emotions Show
We Cry Here
More Than You Know

There Are Terrible Things You Cannot Share
But, Please Through All Things
Unsaid We Sure Do Care

Our Love We Send You Is Real
The "Thank You's Aren't Enough
Be Safe God Loves You
He Will Guide You and Be With You
He Loves You Very Much

NO CLOCK IN HEAVEN

If there ever was time in heaven
There wouldn't be enough to go around
For God never sleeps
He's on watch all the time
To make sure we are all safe and sound

Earths time seems to go so slowly
When we are hurried
When we are enjoying the moment
We would like to make it last

How can life are measured with hands
Hours moving to a rhythm sometimes chimes

How then do we measure time?
Does it matter?
The world began, the world will end
No time can tell when we've reached
The top of the ladder

IMBALANCE

The scale is tipped nothing balances
The mind works overtime as if
Time has stopped

Circles are grooved by running the same way
Connecting the beginning
To the end at time without a move

Thinking gets cluttered
Surrounding oneself with confusion
Words are muttered
How does one control thoughts
That are traveling with speed
No-one can really fill your needs

Frustrations set in one cannot explain
What happens within?
Why does one keep repeating?
What one feels deleting?

It begins all over again
Asking the same questions
How can anyone help?
When one keeps going the right direction

Repeativness of the same feeling doing
Things you don't mean to
Try and stop these feelings altogether
Hope to God for healing

Things worsen when the fighting begins
I believe one thought is right when
Opposition is again relived

Thoughts are controlled by Meds
Without them nothing gets better
Feelings get rambled
Then the mind gets scrambles

Counseling maybe therapist are needed
To vent the hurtfulness
Well hopefully all of this will help
We can live life to the fullest

LOVE AMONG US

No need for competition
Smile and lend a hug
Apply the ointment for the healing
Hold tightly to Peace and love

But quiet the lashes hit us
Humiliation for our mistakes
Quickened smirks that cut us
Hateful people who ridicule all
Their razor blades slice us until we fall

Will the guilty save themselves?
Before the end has come of our universe
And the world?

Will they stop blaming someone else?
For their guilt?
Will they learn to love themselves?
Instead of hating others?

Let God lead you in everything
Not part time but full time
Are there benefits with this job?
Yes God is working Full time
Yet we receive the benefits
Now this is truly love

SOMETIMES

Sometimes we cry to cleanse our
Burdened thoughts of being apart

Sometimes there is commotion
Never a quiet moment
Sometimes things calm down
There is silence, too much silence
One wishes for more commotion

Sometimes we are so sad
When times don't seem so bad
Sometimes things seem so difficult
Even with all the direction we had

Sometimes no matter what we do
The day seems so unwound
Sometimes we find the happiness within
The day. Is the memory to be found?

Sometimes the happiness within the day
Is such a memory to be found?
Sometimes we need each other more
Then we really know
Sometimes we have great days
Others may be bad days all in a row

Sometimes we just need to be quiet within ourselves
Sometimes we gather those good times
To put them safely away
Reminding us on what shelf
They're on so our love will never end

ALL THAT'S THERE

All that's there it came from where?
There isn't room for reasons anywhere
Reasons are many through our days
Who gets through it there?
Praise God for all who care

Our lives are where? Over there?
Where is there? A great place
Pray if you dare
Where? Anywhere ask for forgiveness
Also Peace to be in Gods care

See the stripes red white and blue?
Do you know what the flag stands for?
How selective are you then? How did we get there?
What's the world made of?

How selective are you then?
How did we get here?
What's the world made of?

Can you see the wind blow without trees?
And things that blow?
Can you touch a piece of the sky?
Where? See all that's there?

SHARING, CARING, AND LEARNING

Well you think you had it bad?
Man when I was growing up
Sometimes I was rather sad

You start out as a toddler
Crying when you need attention
Going through normality's in life
Were questions which way?
Which dimension?

Then there comes another stage
With a new brother or sister
Then there's a word called sharing
Giving up things that were once yours alone
Learning not to be greedy
Sharing and pleasing

Sometimes I get plain angry
Because I have to share think of others first
But I don't want to
It's not that I don't care
Now I'm older going through puberty problems
I don't know how to act
Seems as though I'm always wrong
Really given no slack

There are arguments of who is right
Whose wrong isn't there a rule book?
To tell me where I belong?

Now comes the questions
Why can't I stay out late? My friends can
Probably because you're parents care
You need to understand

Well do you ever think I'll ever get my way?
There will be consequences
I know I will have to pay

Won't I ever learn to think things out?
Before hurtful things? I hate to say
Mom and Dad were right. Because
That thought really bites like a sting

O.K.I have accepted these thoughts now
But cripes it wasn't easy
I guess parents know what they're doing
After all they are so pleasing

I guess I owe Mom and Dad lot
I took advantage of situations
In a short slot
I have to say thank you
For all of the support
Boy I sure was in the hot seat
Sometimes on the davenport

But we all know eventually
Things will all work out
Butting heads, locking horns, shouting,
Disagreeing only leaves me lonely

ALONE TO POUT

If I'd only listen to hear the loving phrases
I wouldn't have to apologize, I wouldn't
Go through such mazes

But now all is worked out
Normal voices we hear
I love you son/daughter these
Thoughts we will always hold dear

CORONA VIRUS

The Corona Virus has now hit
Everyone is panicking
Now everything is off the shelves
Nothing's left not even a little bit

Toilet paper, paper towels, and sanitizers
Are all gone none in sight
People are hoarding and greedy
It's such a sad sight

Meats and the freezer section
Were hit too milk and dairy products
There is nothing left of a selection

People, People why are you panicking?
Why are you not leaving anything?
For anyone who needs it?
Everything is lacking

Not even a baby wipe or diapers
Are left on the shelf
What will mothers do?
There is nothing else

Now all the stores are closing early
Supplies are in demand
Hoarders take heed
Limits are at hand

Now stop panicking and live a normal life
It's like the flu
The shelves weren't bare then!
Because it wasn't anything new

Let's all work together now
Not to panic you know?
Be in harmony, love each other
Share and be kind to one another

Share this poem with everyone
It is needed badly
Take care of yourselves and others also
God loves us all very gladly
Written March 16, 2020

SNOW

Snow so white so very bright
Glimmering on the branches of trees
Sometimes heavy sometimes light
It accumulates with all its might

Just a dusting at times is nice
God gives this beauty all for free
At times water turns into ice
Icicles form in forms of spears
They're beautiful hanging there off the roof
Sometimes icicles trees dripping off like tears

It's gorgeous sparkling during the day
Not so pretty when the day is gray
Snow so fluffy when one walks it blows
When it's heavy and lake effect
The wind kicks in and freezes your nose

Some days are way below zero
Keep warm and bundled up
Don't try and be a hero

Children play outside they love to chat
They build snowmen and igloos on the lawn
Snow is so amazing when it's thick and packed
When children make things it looks
As though it was made by pros
Jack Frost is so cold nipping at your nose

So when it snows always know
Get shovels ready
For inches will grow
Sometimes snow so deep one
Needs a snow blower

Now it's time to play
Only now we can play without delay
Water turning to icicles

Enjoy the snow it's only one season
Next you'll have shovels out
For the same reason
Happy Snow Day!

THE STORM THAT BLEW OVER

Boy what a day now mind you
The only hurt you feel is
Because you let it

I've been slapped with words
Cried so hard my daughter joined me
Because of both of our words

The day did not turn out as expected
No sleep for one, no sleep
No sleep for the other
With an ear infection

My little one did cry with fright
He said "Grandma Will you be alright?"
The younger of the two was laughing
Giggling because he was too you
Young to understand verbal lashings

When this storm of emotions passed over
Boy did it rain
There were hugs and apologies over and over

Now the confusion of clouds have passed
We are at one level and
Can laugh
Oh what a joy it is to enjoy grandchildren
They'll love you no matter what
Undying love, gentle, and loving
Hugs and kisses and a sweet touch

TRYING TO SURVIVE

Time passes oh so slowly
When one is oh so lonely
Pain seems forever
Tears feel forever flowing

Life is not fair for any reason
Things taken that are not by choice

We are not in control
Someone else took away our rights
One cannot speak their mind
Words said before are now a crime

Discrimination in every way
Only spoken differently even
Though it's betrayal
Too many cars/vehicles of all sorts on roads
A city this size cannot hold

Gas prices soaring to unbelievable prices
Does anyone want to take control back?

It's been taken we need to fight back
It's a war of sorts not by choice
But everyone should STOP for one minute
No movement, no sounds, just quietness
One minute to actually see what is happening

Loneliness, people are poor, funds running out
For emergency help
Prices going up, wages not enough,
Double income is forced, childcare needed
For working people

Half the check goes right to the daycare
Making one feel they shouldn't have worked
In the first place
No gain, it feels like minimum wage?
Who could even live on that then?
A single parent surely can't
Why are people so selfish?

The rich get richer,
The poor get poorer
Life is so out of order

Think with your mind
Be very kind
Then everything
Will start to unwind

Thank you lord for all you have given
I'm sure a lot of us will see you in heaven

THE NEW BABY

Congratulations! Are in order
To a lucky couple
Having a baby is so exciting
To you both
Excitement won't burst your bubble

The newness is of the unknown
To you and your first bundle
May your pathways be of clear sailing
May you never stumble

We want to find the perfect card
To fit this special occasion
But we thought being here in person
We'd have a special celebration

So here's to heath and happiness
Of every given moment
Say loving words always to each other
Life will be so much easier
That way won't it?

We care about you very much
So with the growth of the little one
Sometime soon
With months flying by
The excitement will grow by leaps and bounds

But when the baby is finally here
You both will be very proud
Now we call you parents
Of a newborn child
Aunts, Uncles, Cousins, and Grandparents
A new life accepted With a smile

GONE FEELINGS

Feelings of happiness
Feelings of joy
Feelings of excitement
Are all gone

Feelings of love
Feelings of embracing
Feelings of hugs
Feelings of kisses
No need to feel strong

Feelings of togetherness
Feelings of going out
Feelings of enjoying friendships
Feelings of touch
All have disappeared

Feelings all together
Are no longer felt
Everything is gone

Everything is lost
Can't afford the cost

No efforts are being made
To find a job on his part
Since he quit his job
At the Mini Mart

My love of my van will now be gone
All things I treasure
Will be pawned

For all of these things I have worked hard for
It no longer matters
The future needs to be prepared for

I may be alone
The gone feelings are here
I am empty and numb

I have to go on
One way or another
Go it alone if I have to
But the feelings are gone

Respect is gone
Belief is gone
Holding on is gone
How can I continue to go on?

There won't be food
Nor bills paid
Rent will be late
Then eviction notice will wait
No house then
No warmth all that I treasured Is gone

The care for the animals needs
Are all gone
We'll lose them too
Everything I hold dear
Is now forever gone

REMEMBERING MOM

My tears they flow daily now
As I know what to expect
My heart aches so badly
For me to recollect

My mother is paying the price of life
Which we know will end with death
It freezes my soul and its dam
Hard to accept

When I finally catch my breath from crying
Another memory floods my mind
I ask myself how women can
Suffering so much can manage to
Still be so kind

I'd rather me you'd burden
Than this woman's righteous soul
But we know a powerful God
That you take all control
How can one accept this affliction?
It's so hard to share the pain
The days ahead and
Possibly remission

Now there are few phone calls
Visitors are few
It seems the walls are getting higher
We ask you God what we shall do.

Some are afraid to close their eyes
The weariness is now showing
The numerous things needing done
Are growing

Lord steer our hearts in the right direction
Show us where we should be heading next
Help us understand that you are our God
That you will not tolerate rejection

Only God is in charge of prayers
Of which we are aware
Let us bow our heads now

Help this family hold together"
In this time of need

Oh hear our cries of plead
For we love this woman so
We are asking for a miracle
From heaven to earth below

Ready Lord?
Keep us on the wings of angels
Gliding peacefully through the sky

We are asking for a miracle
From heaven to earth below
Hear our cries of Plead
We are praying for a miracle
For this woman we now pray

SISTERS

For the times we've shared
Good and bad up and down plead
For we love this woman so

Sometimes smile are upside down
Hectic days filled with all kinds of moods
Laughing, crying, smiles, and confusion
Everyday life sometimes can have
All moods mixed in one
What an intrusion

Money, not enough or short too often
Bills come too quickly collectors don't soften
Upbringing of children
Can be costly and unending
Always needing something
Upon us always depending

No matter what the mood good or bad
When you hurt I am also sad

We share the same no matter what
We are laughing, loving crying our tears
Of happiness always understanding
Because we are sisters

I love you sis if it's any indication
Our life is real not made of Claymation
I truly have the feelings you have
At one time or another
Or any time at all
Pick up the phone and give me a call
Let's be close as sisters should be
My love for you is free no price attached
Now let's see you try and buy something
In this world for that fee! Free

If I didn't care about you and your family
I wouldn't have wrote these verses
Let's hug each other
Forget our troubles and
Cry if we need to
But my love for you you'll never have to purchase
I love you sis Donna

TOXIC PARENTS

Some parents can be toxic
They hold you from your dreams
They never see a problem
With frustrations you scream

Why did you hurt me?
You limited my success
I hadn't any encouragement
Only heart ache and stress

You never said encouraging words
Only negative critical statements
I feel as though you've trapped me
Inside of a glass encasement

My feelings were all bottled up
With pressure so strong it would burst
Even though you controlled my life
Somewhere out there is the life I thirst

You may not think you've done anything wrong
But on the other side of the coin
Is the help you needed for so long
Not help in financing or buying a new car
But a psychologist who will tell you
You've pushed your kids too far

They feel they've had no success
Throughout this horrible torment
But look over there! There's hope
Love and God but, other things are dormant

Toxic is very harmful
Ruining everything in sight
Take a good long look at yourself
You say "wow my life is a fright"

The people who have done this damage
Are in total denial
They think they've done nothing wrong
Like this sort of treatment
Is in style

This in fact is the usual way
Toxic people usually act
Unless these people seek some help
Their lives will continue
Like this that's a fact

A chain has to form with individual counseling
By oneself or a group
Which ever way you choose to council
Each chain link will be
Attached hanging on to each loop

When counseling has been done
Then problems then well be solved
Hopefully all the toxicity
Will diminish and dissolve

WHERE IS CHRISTMAS

The meaning of Christmas is lost somewhere
Out there along the way
Where is Christmas?

The cares of Jesus' birth is forgotten
There are lights decorating homes
Bushes, even trees, walkways
Windows yes even some vehicles too
Where is Christmas?

Very few show the manger seen
More show a jolly fellow
Who brings toys also gifts
To everyone what happened?
Where is Christmas

Christmas should be a time of thanks
For gifts God blessed us with
Not how many presents one received

Each year people spend more money in
Families wouldn't it be wonderful
If we took care of Gods own?
Where is Christmas?

Take a gathering of friends to help someone
Else who has nothing? Give to charity?
Badly needed funds for illnesses!
Where is Christmas

People look around one another do
You see Christmas? Do you buy Christmas?
Do you give Christmas?
We already have Christmas
It's in our hearts
Love is Christmas

Giving our love, a helping hand of goodness
Is Christmas! Do you feel it? Bringing
A smile to those less fortunate
Who are lonely, touching a hand,
Giving a smile to show you really care
That's Christmas
Maybe some day the world will find
The true meaning of Christmas

Please don't take Christ out of Christmas
Without Christ we are of non-existence
We are a blessing from God
Now that's Christmas

THE MIRACLE OF A HUG

Did you ever see a smile disappear
From someone's face?
Where the smiles lines were are
Now an empty space?

A smile turned upside down
Is usually a frown
Which is sadness, pain, tears, and unhappiness?
Feelings so intense one feels down

Finding sympathy or pity isn't
What one wants
Just someone to care and share
The emptiness of a heart

Feelings disappear from the whole
Soul and one is numb
Will there be anyone who understands
Without pressing feelings
Further under their thumb?

Sometimes all it takes is the
Miracle of a hug
Where nobody has to say a word
But feelings built up sure do unplug
Just a smile and a warm feeling
Comes out of this hug

Because someone shows you
They really care and
Want to understand

Someone embracing your soul and
Absorbing all your pain
You come back to reality
Without harsh commands

I find it quite amazing how a word
Doesn't have to be said
A hug says everything without speaking
Then healing begins to repair
The sadness or pain instead

PEOPLE ARE SO CRUEL

Some people are so rude
They speak so cruel
They think they are all so cool

They've nothing else to do but
Spew things about others rolling
Out of their mouths like a spool

Things' going around one listens
To the gossip
Don't forget to put down others
Treat them bad. Lies and truth flip flop

Let's talk about others how they are so wrong
Also unpopular younger people
Just keep on running their jaws
Cannot accept when they're not so strong

Sometimes in ones life all things
Just don't stop there
The judgment day will come
When all things bad said won't compare

The person's jaws that just kept going
About how bad and wrong people were
For what's in store for them
Would not stop God he won't be so nice to liars
For punishment will come to those
Whose lips were town criers

Think about it all you being cruel
Your fight is with God
Think you'll win the duel?

HOUSECLEANING

Housecleaning is not done alone
With bucket mop or broom
It takes a certain gadget
For almost any single room

You have to be an artist
In domestic qualities
Even then results of perfect aims
Are not easy as A, B, C's

You have to have that certain touch
For what ever is in the house
When you challenge dust and dirt
It's like a game of cat and mouse

Each room need noted special care
From ceiling to the floor
A practiced eye will get results
Most any tenant is looking for

Finally when the job is done
That's been accomplished very neat
You can proudly leave another house
That's the cleanest on the street
Written By my Grandfather
Chris Kunstman to me Donna Richter

GIT- ER' DONE USA

Go troops!
Be wise take nothing
By surprise

Be alert! Be safe!
Keep the faith
Communicate

Listen to each other
No matter when the
Call comes take cover!

Some of us are left behind
But, please know
We would proudly stand
In your duty line

Defend our country

Move swift but silently
Beware of traps and gaps

Walk sure footed
Safely on guard
To every moment
That feels it could cause harm

The **USA** is here to back you
We will be rooting for you
Prayers will also come
Until the enemy is down
When the work is done

Pride to the soldiers
Of every command
The enemy knows from
Them what we demand
Written by: A loving mother who's
Son is serving in Iraq n the National Guard
Donna M. Richter

BULLYING

Our world d is such a mess
Fighting and bombing senseless
Deaths and all kids of threats

People can't live a normal life
Whatever normal is it's a fright
We teach our children to get along
Not to fight or hate but be strong

Do you think adults and children alike
Can live a normal life?
With gangs and shootings
Peer pressures explode
Like the tightening of a vice

The pressure is immense now
More rapes and sexual predators
Who will survive these attackers?
More stories for the editors!

Bullying has become fierce it's so bad
Kids as well as adults are afraid it's so sad
So scared that their personality changes
Some go into hiding letting no one in their spaces

The rage is pushed down there's no control panel
People aren't safe at work or school
Now bullies are the ones that rule

They run down or make fun of one so bad
That their life is just nothing but sad
Bullies take control of your life
Some even make people do things that aren't nice
Some even make people do things for a price

Bullying is so bad today at work, at school
Just in general anywhere
They make you feel like a fool

The price of bullying can even be a life
It get's so bad people can't take it anymore
Threatened not to tell anyone or pay the price

How very sad when people get away with
Doing these things to others
Most feel like they are being smothered

It's horrible when one hears on the news that
Another person or child has taken their life
All because nobody takes control of these people
Why? Why? Should these people have to suffer
Because of all the darkness that lurks

This has to be stopped! Please someone help!
Have God take control of this please
If nobody can take control of this please
Let the hand above us take the lead

STOP THE BULLYING in our schools, at work
Also on the internet
Please hold your heads high
Talk to someone who will listen into your lives
They will not pry

Let no one want to harm themselves
Because of something said or done
These bullies will be dealt with
There won't be anymore harm coming to anyone

There will be consequences you who are bullying
That should have done before
But now you will be the ones suffering
Because now we are going to even the score

PLEASE STOP BULLYING! NO BULLYING ALLOWED
STOP BULLIES ALL AROUND AND
PEACE WILL BE FOUND

NATURE

Isn't it beautiful?
All that comes along with it
So many colors and shapes
Such beauty all around

Sad to say people litter
They throw garbage around
Making nature look awful bitter

How can people do this?
To such beauty we are blessed with
People pick up after yourselves!
Where we can reconnect it

Clouds in the sky
Trees of all beauty
Keeping the beauty
After all is our duty
God has given us freely all of nature
On this beauty let us feature

So when you are out and about
Take a good long look
You won't see this in a book

DEAR GOD

Dear God I would like to send you a letter
But there isn't any way to send it
It would say "Thank you God for all
You've done for me to make my life better"

I talk with you every day
There's no cost for it that we would pay
Just a minute ago I was praying
All about the disaster we are saying
Dear God protect us be by our side
With this prayer I will abide

How will we overcome COVID-19 today
Many people are very sick on this very day
We have to practice social distancing now
Also proper hand washing we need to remember how
Dear God I know you are here with me
I feel your presence with myself and family
Keep us safe from all harm
Amen God no need for alarm

PEOPLE

People are running around everywhere
Don't go too close if you dare
Practice social distancing and good hand washing
"Don't touch your face" they are demanding

People are taking things off the shelves
There's nothing left for anyone else
People are panicking, hoarding food and supplies
Nothing left what a surprise
People, now the stores have strict limit
Two per person no more or you're in trouble
We used to have no problem buying doubles

People, what a mess you have caused
This hurts like a cut without any gauze
Why are you hoarding and leaving none
People, you are hurting us in more ways then one

People let God be control
Of this mess you have caused us
People, God already knows how this will end
For on Gods help we do depend

ISOLATION

We are all in isolation in our city
Everyone has to stay home
We're all going to get giddy

Crime will go up that's a fact
People aren't working that's exact
Businesses are closed for now
People aren't getting paid
Too much Wow

This will be going on for months we're told
Stay away from people anxiety unfolds
Cabin fever is on the rise
Well that should come to no surprise

"We're all in this together" folks
This is not a hoax
As time goes by all life will resume
We hope our life it doesn't consume
Now that we are all together
People will get frustrated with each other
"Let me out I want to see my sisters and brothers
Let God take control now
For he'll show us all how
Put your faith in him
Then life won't seem so grim

HUSBAND

I love my husband very much
It's a feeling you just can't touch
There's a thrill of love in his eyes
Don't say hurtful things to each other
Your relationship will be compromised

I know one day God you will
Take me from him or him from me
I pray not soon on bended knee

My husband is my friend and companion
Our love for each other we've been handed
We've been blessed together for forty six years
With that there's been heartache and tears

God you've helped us to work it all out
Then yeah we're friends again
That's what I'm talking about
God puts us together for a reason
For any time any season

Now we are close together all the time
Sometimes we wonder what would happen
If we lose one another
I think that would be a crime

Love us lord keep us together
As long as possible we pray
Keep us near you every day

For if you decide we ever will part
We know it will take a piece of our hearts
Let us love each other stronger every day
For this free love
We'll never have to pay Amen

LIFE'S WORRIES

Oh boy, oh boy,
Life deals us such a hand
Creditors wanting money, problems at work
How do we take a stand?
Bills overflowing and worries that builds up
Can't make ends meet
It's a blow to the gut

Is there understanding or just priorities
I guess their concern is just money
What's owed that's the majority
What happened to peace and understanding?

That green paper sure becomes demanding
How do we grow and populate more money
We already work so hard
We're beat and it's not funny

Seems as though the problems grow
They hardly get resolved
The next day there's less money
So more problems are added
Seems as though nothing is dissolved

We try and play catch up with bills
Worries and all concerns of life
Seems as though we're handed more stresses
Not enough pardons just another
Twist of the knife

How do we clear these clouds before our eyes
We blink and the haze remains
Please clear up these clouds of life
Before we awaken and rise

There is an answer but all
Of your patience it will take
Give the worries to God
Close your eyes, listen to the
Soothing sounds of the lake

The water rolls like thunder
Splashing over everything in sight
Like creditors give me money
You haven't any rights

Somehow we find strength and patience
From where does it come?
We all know this answer hang on
To all given us from above

Help us ask this almighty one
Give us your hand open our hearts
Our minds then and only then
Your will shall be done

KIDDO'S

Kiddos everywhere now it seems to be
No school, no work. Close quarters it seems
School work, laundry, housekeeping too
Makes one wonder will they ever go back to school

It's so sad because the kiddos can't play with friends
When will this pandemic come to an end?
Kiddos find it hard some too young to young
Understand

Kiddos can't go anywhere why? They demand
Why do we have to stay in mom and dad?
It's hard to explain to them
How very sad

Kiddos make you laugh at their silliness
Brings the day back to all its business
Kiddos are loving, all the time spent with them
Some are content but, others aren't but do pretend

Kiddos, kiddos what can we do
To make you happy while out of school?
Watch a movie, spend time together
Takes you back and helps one remember

Kiddos are my life now
I missed so much I don't remember how
Now we are getting so close knit
But have to have our space a little bit

Kiddos, kiddos we love you
At times it's hard for you too
Let us enjoy our time we have
God protect us on our behalf
Amen

FRIENDS

Friends are very trusting to me
Friends are always friendly and friends are free
Friends are always on your side
When disagreements come
Friends know exactly where you're coming from
Friends are considerate and kind
Friends are not selfish
But give me piece of mind
Friends are always there for you
Friends are friends always this is true

Friends are human too
Friends disagree with you that's true
Friends work things out with friends that's for sure
Friends depend on our friendship no departure

Friends are friends forever and always
All the years through
Friends laugh and cry hurt and feel low
Even when it feels like a blow

Friends are amazing don't you think?
Friends hang on to us
Like a chain link

Friends are sweet and understanding
All the time
Friends will stay with you like the spin of a dime
Friends love each other to pieces
Friends Yes friends without any leases

Friends, friends, friends, we will be forever
Friends we shall always be together
Friends to the end
Friends yes on us you can depend

BUSY

Busy, busy, busy so much to do
I don't know if I'll get
Everything done before the day is through

Wash the dishes, sweep the floor
After that there will be more
Do the laundry, make the bed
Don't forget to put on the bed spread

Bake the bread, cook dinner too
Isn't there enough to do?
Wash the dishes, clean the table
Do all the above if you are able

The day goes fast
Time flies by it doesn't last
Keep yourself moving all day long
Isn't this where we belong?

Hurry, hurry, do the dusting
Don't let anything get too musty
Clean the windows, wipe the walls
Don't clutter so anybody falls

Now the end of the day has come
Where did the day go? Where did it come from
Everyone is settled in for the night
It's quiet now so say goodnight

CATS

Cats so beautiful just look at those eyes
Striped coats spotted coats different
Colors what a surprise

Pouncing, running, playing
With balls of yarn
They're never boring
Some cats were born in a barn

The claws you have to watch
Be careful you don't get scratched
Some cats are fat some are skinny
Some are full grown some are mini

Coats of all colors and spots
Some even have polka dots
Tiger striped, cow design on some
Some have rarities where does it come from

God sure does have a special hand
He designs things upon demand
All he has to do is say what he
Wants and it shall be done
It's always amazing where
Our world comes from

Thank you God for all you
Have given us
In your name we do trust
Miracles are everywhere one looks
Even words printed in a book

CARDINALS

Cardinals are so beautiful all red feathers
Such beauty like looking through infrared
Gorgeous colored or reds outlined with black
Just wonderful to look at

Pretty as they sit on a branch of a tree
They are so adorable and free
Flying freely through the sky
When one hears them sing
They say "oh my"

Such a beautiful song they chirp
You can hear them throughout the neighborhood
The sounds you hear from them chirp, chirp
There is no greater God then good
For who else would give us such beauty
Then the one who made us you and me

Thank you God for all you've
Blessed us with
In these hard times help us get
Through them and quick
Amen

BROTHER

My brother is so special to me
Even if we have a code word it's funny
Calling all cars it's your sister here
Calling my brother who I hold so dear

Remember the days… we talk about
The years gone past without a doubt
Sharing times of the past
How life goes by so fast

Every time we talk on the phone
You leave me laughing
The flooded memories are a crashing

Good times, bad times we've
Made it through
Still thinking of them makes one blue

All in all we've lived our lives
Grown up some cries some smiles
Angry times sad times we made it
It was hard it just took a bit

Now we are all grown up with families
With grandchildren
Our life today we are a handling
We call each other once a week
Talking to you is so sweet
Brother I love you more and more
As life goes on we make phone calls and know
We love each other now and forever

So when you hang up the phone
Our conversation stays in my mind
I take it with me for
When I need to unwind

Thanks for being there brother
For we are there for one another
For all the years we have left here
We don't know but until then
Then I'll hold you dear
Your sister Donna

BAKING

Baking is fun and great to eat
All the ingredients you must beat
Make sure all is blended well
Secret ingredients you cannot tell

Mix the ingredients blend them together
This recipe I should remember
Whirring beaters beat the eggs
Don't stand too long you'll get wobbly legs

Get the pans ready grease and flour
You'll have to bake this for at least an hour
Don't forget to preheat the oven
Set the temperature you'll have at least a dozen

If you're making a cake
It will take longer to bake
Cakes take longer to rise
But they're delicious that's no surprise

When the timer goes off
Then everything is done
Remove it immediately from the oven

Let it cool do the dishes
Clean up time wash the beaters
Don't touch anything yet
Don't be cheaters

When it's time for dessert
Everyone is happy
You've worked so hard
You feel like a nappy
Oh no! You cannot rest
For this is going to be the best

WALKING

Walking can be fun
If you're walking with someone
You get to chat about goings on
Look at nature are there ducks on the pond?

Sometimes, you see others walking
Some alone, some have friends and are talking
If you're alone just look at nature
There's beauty everywhere, even creatures

Don't walk too fast
You'll get out of breath
Just walk at a comfortable speed
You're walk will last

I have a neighbor I walk with
She's so awesome always interesting I insist
We walk twice a day first walk a one
The other at six
All the way we do talk

Find someone to walk with today
Practice social distancing or you'll pay
Keep safe always of danger
Never feed information to a stranger

We end our walk with
"See you later"
Until then you can read the paper

SHOPPING

Go out shopping if you dare
Usually everything is scarce
People are hoarding even with a limit
Other people need it
Why don't you share it

Some people have to go without
They'll be hungry without a doubt
Let's sop and share what is there
There's a limit now you have to share
Any store you go to
There is a line to wait in
Just be patient soon the line will
Shorten and you can begin
Begin to be waited on or give
You a sanitized cart
What they are doing
I think is pretty smart

Do your shopping on down time
That way you'll get what you need
Without a crime

Be safe shoppers
Wear protection
You never know what's
Coming in your direction

Leave the store with
A smile on your face
Feel good about yourself
At least you were safe
This was written during the Corona Virus Scare

STAYING AT HOME

Staying at home can be pretty hard
One thinks too much
Your feelings are jarred
Communication is what it takes
To keep your life going take a ride by the lake

Busy yourself with
Something to do
There's always something
This is true

Do the chores
Get them done
I know sometimes
It's not fun
It will keep your sanity
Don't forget to dust the vanity

Dust the dust away
From everything in sight
Otherwise everything
Will look like a fright

Once the day comes to and end
You can now go to bed
Say your prayers and say Amen

THE END

The end the end yes the
End has come
For this book anyway
The time has come

Others will be on their way
How soon? Well it's hard to say
Maybe a week a month later
Hard to say right now
Depends on the illustrator

When shall I write again?
Probably tomorrow
If I don't I'll be in sorrow

It's fun to write
If you know how
As a matter of fact
I can write right now

`Have to put on my
Thinking cap
It's not time to
Take a nap

So where will the
Words come from?
The mind you say?
Like the beat of a drum

So now I shall say
It's the end
You'll hear from me again
Just in time to say you again?

So long so long
So long everyone
I'll see you soon
On that you can count on

Be safe keep
Your distance
Protect yourself
Also your resistance

Don't forget to
Read my next book
I don't want it
To sit in a nook

Pick it up please
Read all the words
On this book
You can endure

Goodbye for now everyone
I hope you've enjoyed
This book I hope you had fun